YOUR KNOWLEDGE HAS VALUE

Aldridge Menzel

How well placed Apple is to sustain its recent success in the Consumer Electronics Industry

GRIN Verlag

Bibliografische Information der Deutschen Nationalbibliothek:

Die Deutsche Bibliothek verzeichnet diese Publikation in der Deutschen National-
bibliografie; detaillierte bibliografische Daten sind im Internet über http://dnb.d-
nb.de/ abrufbar.

Imprint:

Copyright © 2013 GRIN Verlag GmbH
Druck und Bindung: Books on Demand GmbH, Norderstedt Germany
ISBN: 978-3-656-62556-8

This book at GRIN:

http://www.grin.com/en/e-book/270835/how-well-placed-apple-is-to-sustain-its-
recent-success-in-the-consumer

How well placed Apple is to sustain its recent success in the Consumer Electronics Industry

Table of Contents

Introduction

Apple Inc. has been into the electronics business since some decades in the industry. It had built its place in the markets, all over the world through its dynamic strategies that focused on quality and innovation. Apple Inc. has made progress from being a loss making company to being the biggest company in the electronics industry with incredibly high revenues and profit margins.

The assignment is going to be based upon Apple Inc.'s case study and its journey as a whole to becoming a successful company. It will highlight the strategies adopted by the company, their adoption of the environmental changes and how it used these dynamics for its own benefits. Apple Inc.'s vision, mission and beliefs as an organization, the company's strengths and weaknesses have been highlighted in the following assignment.

Also discussed in the assignment are the changing business and competitive environment and its impact on the company, the challenges it faces in such an environment and, the strategies it adopts to excel in this field. The structures that the company follows, the systems on which it is based on and other operational efficiencies, all play a major role in the Apple growth story. The company is known for innovation and quality. In spite of the premium prices, the company has almost a maximum market share to it and continues to grow up the success ladder with its ever evolving product line which is a mixture of quality, innovation and highly detailed mechanics.

Apple continues to not only survive, but excels in the electronics market which, is becoming more and more competitive by the day.

About Apple Inc

Apple Inc. is a multinational born in America which, is involved into designing, development and sales of consumer electronic products, computer software and hardware and personal computing. Headquartered in California, it was founded on the 1st of April, 1976 by Steve Jobs. Also accompanying him in foundation were Ronald Wayne and Steve Wozniak Initially it was found to develop personal computers and later expanded to include other consumer electronic items in its product line. It is spread across 14 different countries around the globe and is present by means of around 408 retail outlets which sell Apple products. (Kim, 2012)It is the largest retailer for music in the world through its iTunes store. Apple Inc.'s headquarters are:

Apple Campus

One Infinite Loop

Cupertino

California, U.S.A.

The company has around 72,800 full-time employees who are permanents and 3,300 full-time employees who are temporary. Apple was ranked sixth in the list of Fortune 500 companies in 2013, from being 11th place in 2012. Its revenue is about US$ 156 billion. (Goldman, 2012)

Mission and Vision

As a company that believes so firmly in innovation and quality rather than simply sales and lower costs.Apple's mission statement as reported in the 1980s, by Steve Jobs, was 'To make a contribution to the world by making tools for the mind that advance humankind'. 'Man is the creator of change in this world' was also reported to be among one of the mission statements. (BLODGET, 2013)

Apple Inc. has had a strong value system and work culture. Their belief in quality work and doing everything right has led them to be one of the most admired companies in the world.

According to the current CEO of Apple Inc., Mr. Tim Cook, the values on which Apple as a company is based on are:

- Making great products.
- Keeping it simple, rather than complicating it.
- Making and owning the primary and basic technologies used to develop their products.
- Being a participant of only those markets, where the company feels, it can make a valuable contribution.
- Focusing on only those projects that are meaningful and important to the company, rather than going in for thousands of other projects.
- Deeply collaborating and cross-pollinating across the companies various groups, allowing them to innovate in better ways which gives them an edge over other competitors.
- Anything below the level of excellence is not settled for, for every group within the company.
- Being honest to admit to mistakes and courageous to make positive changes.

Product line

Apple's product line has been ranging right from its initiation. Its development from Apple II in 1977, which was a successful micro computer has come a long way by way of product innovation and technological advancement. Its breakthrough was achieved by the invention of the Macintosh personal computer in 1984. Followed by that were PowerBook 100, a track ball laptop launched in 1991, the iMac G3 Desktop Computer, the iPod in 2001, the iPod mini in 2004, iPod shuffle in 2005, iPod nano, also in 2005, the MacBook in 2006 which, was known to be the best Macintosh in history, the iPhone in 2007, iPod touch in 2007, iPhone 3G in 2008, showcasing its features of GPS, the MacBook Air in 2008 known for its light weight, portability and sophisticated design and high performance, followed by iPhone 3GS which was an upgrade to its previous version in terms of design and some other voice features, followed by another breakthrough in computing by the launch of iPad in 2010, which was Apple's line of computer tablets, followed by iPod touch 4G in 2010 too, the iPhone 4 in 2011 with better features that involved video calling and FaceTime, better design and technology, followed by iPad 2 and iPhone 4S in 2011, iPad 3 in 2012, iPhone 5, iPad touch 5G, iPad Mini also in 2012. Also, Apple launched a new Mac Pro, iPad Air, iPhone 5 S- claimed to be 'the most forward-thinking phone in the world' and the iPhone 5C-claimed to be 'the most colourful iPhone yet' in 2013. (PIERONI, 2013)

Market Share

Apple Inc. is the second largest information technology company in the whole world in terms of revenue following Samsung Electronics. It is the third largest mobile phone manufacturer following Samsung and Nokia. Apple is the highest traded company on exchange, in the whole world in terms of market capitalization. Its market value is about US$ 415 billion.

Other Achievements

The company was named as 'the most Admired Co.' in the USA in the year 2008 by Fortune magazine and that in the world from 2008 to 2012. In 2013, the Omnicom Group's 'The best Global Brand's report, the brand became the most valuable in the world, overtaking Coca Cola for the title. (Focus, 2013)

Apple Inc.: Growth strategy and Case Analysis

The case talks about how Apple as a company has evolved over the years from the time of its inception to present day. The Apple success story has been contributed to a great extent by its products like iPods and iPhones. Having announced a sale of 200 million iPods which had been in its 8th year since its launch and 2 billion applications sold for the iPhone which was a product in its second year from its launch, the Apple success story had started to take form. However during the period from 2001, as the US economy and slowly even European economies were sliding into recession, the company's sales were drastically affected, making it dependent on business and professional markets. (Pearce, 2008). To overcome this crisis, Apple Inc. strategized its product lines to improve their market share. Coming up with new innovative products had always been the company's strategy. Being the only one in the consumer electronics industry that designs and manufactures the whole personal computer, incorporating its innovative design and technology, the company excelled in getting itself uniquely positioned in the market against its competitors. Its unique software, ease of use, graphics and media technology made the products desirable in the market. It believes in constant development and innovation and highlights product quality, innovation in design, and availability of software, product features, reliability, consumer loyalty, corporate reputation, service and support and marketing and distribution excellence.

Apple's targeted customer segments are:

1. Business
2. Creative Professionals
3. Education
4. High-end consumers

Apple mainly catered to the first two segments before the launch of iPod, after which the client base shifted majorly to education and students. The entry of Apple into consumer products made it more visible and desirable among consumers, rather than only among professionals and businesses. (Sadeghi, 2012)

In order, to enter the digital consumer product market, Apple had to face tough competition since the market had several leading players in companies like Sony, Panasonic, LG, etc. However, identifying opportunities helped Apple gain a tremendous leap in its market share. The music player market was relatively not developed and whatever products were available, had flaws. Apple seized this opportunity to offer quality in an extremely innovative way. 'Music on the move' was chosen by Apple as a strategy, and was one of the hidden demands unknown yet among the masses. Although it had been tapped by Sony through its launch of the Walkman and the Diskman. However, the problem with these devices was that only limited music could be carried with them. Although mp3 players and hard drive players were available they came at a high price. Apple had always entered the markets with premium prices. It identified the factors important to the product were design, size, capacity, battery life, software and download facility. At Apple, the unique strategy of out-to-in design is used. Hiring the right people, with the right ideas, at the right time, is important and hence Apple hired Tony Fadell of Philips, who had an idea for the development of just the kind of mp3 that was needed. Apple's ipod offered 1000 songs in your pocket, which helped it to achieve a market share of about 82 percent by 2004. The iTunes accounted for 87% of all legal music download in the USA. Apple had always aimed for smaller, simpler, more features and less expensive, business mantra for its products.

Apple also tapped the low-end market, which it had never done so far, through its iPod Shuffle. The company had now a dominant product line which had excelled in quality, price and range.

To tap the features of internet connectivity and telephone, the company launched the iPhone. Upgrading its products to include 3G connectivity, video, Wifi, GSM, Bluetooth, downloading data at a better speed, made way for better performance of the products and better consumer experience. The iPhone managed to tap about twenty five percent of the smart phone product market, giving tough competition to Blackberry and Nokia.

The next big thing from Apple was the launch of the iPad which was its computer tablet. It was a portable computer which enabled easy share and viewing of photos, videos, download content, read the newspapers, browse the web, and run other basic computer applications. Another important entry into the Digital Hub Strategy by Apple was the launch of its iBookStore, which allowed the user to download e-books and use the iPad as an e-book reader. The competition it faced were mainly from the Sony e-reader and Kindle from Amazon.

Apple's pricing strategy has always been to enter at a high price, offering quality, and making it available in terms of volumes to maximum of its target markets. Once the volumes increase, the company relaxes the prices. Its focus on quality and innovation have led to great acceptance of the company among its target consumers.

Competition

Apple Inc., the leading consumer electronics company in the world faces stiff competition in the industry from several big players, with the advancement and easy accessibility to technology and information. Over the years, with increase in consumer electronic markets, there has been robust competition from several players in respect to products, innovation, volumes, market share and price sensitivity.

It has faced stiff competition from Windows, right from the time of its early days in case of its computer markets. The computer industry can said to be a monopolistic structure. The entry barriers are low and there are differentiations with regards to products of each firm. This means each firm ideally would be getting a small part of the market share.

Also there are less number of suppliers which means there is low bargaining power for the manufacturers of the product as a whole. Apple here had an advantage, since it manufactured all of the parts that were required to be built for their product, in-house. This helped them gain an edge over other competitors in terms of quality management, innovation in design and advancement in research. Although due to the presence of a lot of competitors, low market share, low margins due to high cost of production, Apple faced a crisis during 2001 and had only 3% market share. Also Apple faced stiff competition for operating systems from Microsoft Windows which had a market share of about 80%. To top this, the switching cost from Microsoft Windows to Mac OS was high, due to the premium prices charged by Apple. Also the impact was more since there was a migration in the demands of personal computers from the developed to the developing countries such as China. (Sadeghi, 2012)

Apple responded to this need of innovation in technology by looking to enter into the consumer market and smartly identifying the underdeveloped portable music industry. It identified the factors that were needed for a product to be successful and that of quality and launched the iPod and its various upgrades.

With the advent of technology, outburst of information technology, consumer electronic products became available at much cheaper prices, and with a range of differentiations. Players like Sony, Samsung, LG, etc. tapped the low-end and middle class markets offering low price quality products.

From the rise of Apple in 2001, towards recession while other competitors faced vulnerability, Apple's sales increased and it led to a healthy growth due to its market segmentation and innovative technology.

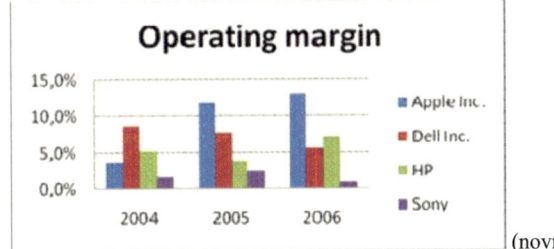

(novriansyah, 2009)

Political Factors

Political factors that most affected Apple was the entry of China into WTO. This opened new avenues for the industries to take advantage of low investment and cheap labour to lower their cost and improve their operating efficiencies. Apple had to respond to this opportunity to keep in line with its competitors who also had the same opportunity available, else it would have been at a disadvantage.

Social Factors

Over time, the social life-style of people has undergone a drastic change. With more and more consumers becoming tech-savy, easy availability of electronic items, which have made life sufficiently easier, Apple has been on the go to innovate and offer premium quality products to the markets. With the creation of a good brand name, Apple has been taking advantage of the sudden technological outburst in today's generation. (novriansyah, 2009)

Micro Environment

Apple's largest competition for operating system comes from Wintel (Windows and Intel), which is a platform that is produced by a large number of firms. The product offering is so similar to that of Apple's with only some differentiation in regards to design, features and the brand name, that it poses a great threat to Apple and its market share holding. The main competitors of Apple are HP, Lenovo, IBM, Fujitsu, Sony, Toshiba, etc. in the computer and operating systems industry.

In the mobile industry the recent developments have seen the players like Samsung become market leaders with their vast range of products, quality, and design, catering to a different segment of market, allowing it to tap the greatest market share for smart phone market. Companies like RIM Blackberry and Nokia, are facing the blow due to lack in updating of their technologies in the smart phone segment. The upcoming promising star is the Google smart phone Nexus, which is giving a tough competition to Apple's iPhone as also Samsung's android smart phones. (Zylla-Woellner, 2013)

With increase in connectivity, mobile internet facilities, Apple has been looking up to innovation to come up with new and different features each time, which helps it stay next to Samsung in the smart phone segment. Apple's launch of iPhone 5S seems to be a promising star and there is great anticipation about its success.

The following chart shows the past market share, near past market shares and the future forecast for smart phones

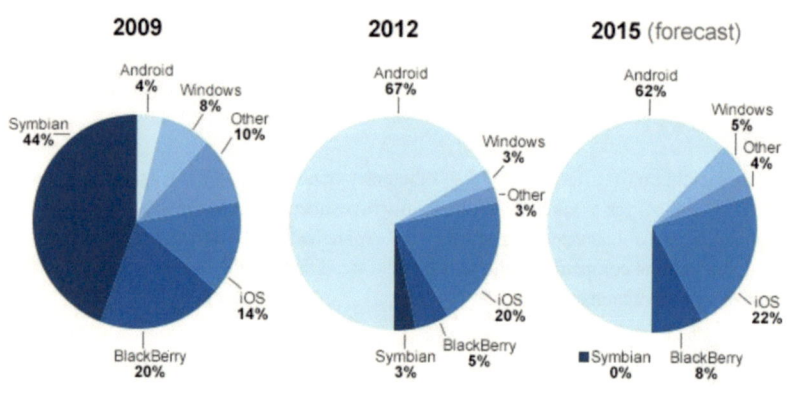

SMARTPHONE MARKET SHARE

SOURCE: ABI RESEARCH; DATA IS BASED ON PHONE SHIPMENTS

(COWLEY, 2013)

Relative Strength and Financial Analysis

Being two greatest competitors in the Smartphone market, the financial analysis of Apple and Samsung has been briefed as below:

In 2012, Samsung sold about 63 million units of Samsung Galaxy and profited more than Google in all of its businesses. However it found it difficult to beat Apple which sold over 5 million Iphone 5S in a weekend. (Focus, 2013)

The investors however are acting dicey post the tax debacle, about its capability to innovate products and designs that help provide it the differentiation that it is known for. The tax debacle involved accusations of Apple taking of tax loop holes and gaining an advantage. However, the CEO was able to well defend the company and this reinforced confidence in Tim Cook's leadership.

The key financial comparison between Samsung and Apple is given as:

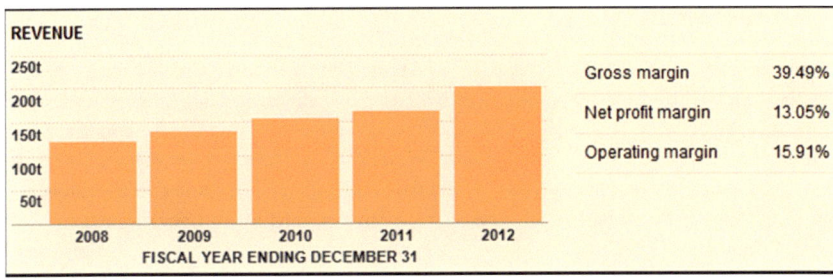

Apple

	2009	2010	2011	2012	Trend	CAGR
Total Revenues	42,905	65,225	108,249	156,508		53.9%
Gross Profit	17,222	25,684	43,818	68,662		58.6%
Operating Income	11,740	18,385	33,790	55,241		67.6%
Net Income	8,235	14,013	25,922	41,733		71.8%

(Focus, 2013)

Samsung

REVENUE		Gross margin	39.49%
		Net profit margin	13.05%
		Operating margin	15.91%

FISCAL YEAR ENDING DECEMBER 31 (2008, 2009, 2010, 2011, 2012)

(Focus, 2013)

These show that on a YOY basis, Apple has grown from US$ 108 billion to US$156 billion which is a significant rise, compared to that of Samsung.

Apple has been beating Samsung's growth in earnings as well (EPS).

However, this growth hasn't materialized to reflect in the share prices. The investor confidence is visible in the stock prices, which support Samsung more than Apple. Samsung has shown a increase in the share price by 10.5%, whereas Apple has fallen by 26%. The forecast analysis for Samsung is positive with an increase in the share price estimated up to 50.2%, a 107.2% high and a negative forecast of only -2.3%. On the other hand Apple's forecast reports a medium of 4.8%, 31.4% high and a negative drop of -27.8%. (Focus, 2013)

However, Apple's strength lies in its ability to control costs. Apple has been able to reduce its COGS from 59.52% to almost 56%. Samsung on the other hand has remained almost the same.

Financially, Apple has better RoA and RoE than reported by Samsung. The RoA of Apple is at 18.91% compared to 15.4% by Samsung. The RoE for Apple is at 33.34% and for Samsung is at 20% only. This shows that the operational efficiencies and financial management of resources is a strength Apple possesses which will help it have an advantage for any future dynamic environmental changes. Apple's strength also lies in its Capital

9

Structure, which makes use of very minimal amount of debt, which reduces its cost and allows it to have a better control over its investors. (Focus, 2013)

It has been argued that Apple is not a sinking Ship. Although its share price has fallen from US$700 in April 2012 to about US$ 540, the launch of iPhone 5S and other promising factors, have started to build investor confidence. It maintains a very healthy balance sheet producing US$50 billion from its cash flows. It is slowly approaching its fair value.

Apple Post Steve Jobs

Steve Jobs was a visionary and extraordinary leader, who could manage to see the big picture in the future and also carve out the details of the same. He knew technology, understood the markets, was skilled at art and could combine all these to form a masterpiece.

However, post Steve Jobs, the former CEO of Apple, Tim Cook was appointed for the post. Apple is a non-conventional company which is based on entrepreneurship, innovation and constant development. This business model helps Apple to grow as long as the company is guided into the right direction. The launch of iPhone 4S and iPhone 5S, yet another iPad, MacBook and more software upgrades reflect that the company's innovativeness is forever growing. Apple's stocks have been increasing and have gone up by 80% surpassing its closest competitor Google.

Apple is preparing to enter the consumer digital product market with yet another product of iTV. It is yet to be seen how far and quickly it will reach the heights without its former leader. However, the current leadership seems promising to keep the flagship of the company soaring high.

The Rise of Xiaomi in China

The Research conducted by consumer insight company Kantar World Panel, reported that Xiaomi, a company found in mainland in 2010, which is able to sell high-specifications on low prices. Its rise is swift and it has become the second largest android seller in China in the third quarter of 2013. It entered the markets at a low price thus conquering a large market share. Apple's sales dropped from 19% to 18%. However, this may be attributed to the consumers waiting for the launch of iPhone 5S and 5c in the last year. (Blum, 2013)

The future

Apple is always in an infinite loop of constant development. Its current management, whether in the markets, or in financials, reflects a positive growth in future since fundamentally its very strong and based on innovation and development.

Bibliography

BLODGET, H., 2013. *Apple's New 'Mission Statement' Is Making People Worry That The Company Has Gone To Hell.* [Online]
Available at: http://www.businessinsider.in/Apples-New-Mission-Statement-Is-Making-People-Worry-That-The-Company-Has-Gone-To-Hell/articleshow/21581584.cms
[Accessed 30 December 2013].

Blum, J., 2013. *Samsung and Xiaomi 'rise in popularity as Apple lags behind'.* [Online]
Available at: http://www.scmp.com/business/companies/article/1367334/samsung-and-xiaomi-rise-popularity-apple-lags-behind
[Accessed 3 January 2014].

COWLEY, S., 2013. *The smartphone market's radical shakeup.* [Online]
Available at: http://money.cnn.com/gallery/technology/mobile/2013/01/29/smartphone-market-share/
[Accessed 4 January 2014].

Focus, G., 2013. *Samsung Vs. Apple - A Financial Comparison.* [Online]
Available at: http://www.nasdaq.com/article/samsung-vs-apple-a-financial-comparison-cm270771
[Accessed 1 January 2014].

Goldman, D., 2012. *Apple's $46 billion sales set new tech record.* [Online]
Available at: http://money.cnn.com/2012/01/24/technology/apple_earnings/index.htm
[Accessed 28 December 2013].

Kim, S., 2012. *Apple (AAPL) Becomes History's Most Valuable Firm on iPhone 5 Rumors.* [Online]
Available at: http://abcnews.go.com/blogs/business/2012/08/apple-aapl-becomes-historys-most-valuable-firm-on-iphone-5-rumors/
[Accessed 30 December 2013].

Mourdoukoutas, P., 2012. *Apple: One Year Into The Post-Steve Jobs Era & One Big Question Remains.* [Online]
Available at: http://www.forbes.com/sites/panosmourdoukoutas/2012/10/04/apple-one-year-into-the-post-steve-jobs-era-one-big-question-remains/
[Accessed 2 January 2014].

novriansyah, n., 2009. *Global Business Environment Analysis of Apple.* [Online]
Available at: http://novriansyah.wordpress.com/2009/10/01/global-business-environment-analysis-of-apple/
[Accessed 3 January 2014].

Pearce, 2008. *Strategic Management.* New York: Tata Mc-Graw Hill.

PIERONI, C., 2013. *Apple's Product Timeline: The Best of the Best.* [Online]
Available at: http://wallstcheatsheet.com/investing/apples-product-timeline-the-best-of-the-

best.html/?a=viewall
[Accessed 2 January 2014].

Sadeghi, S., 2012. *Defensive Strategy – Apple's Overlooked Key to Success.* Berlin: epubli GmbH.

Zylla-Woellner, J., 2013. *Global economic Development within the Scope of Apple Inc..* s.l.:Grin.